Reading Well
2

**John Cooper
and
George Livingstone**

Oliver & Boyd

The author and publishers are grateful to the following for permission to reproduce extracts from the publications listed:

Chatto & Windus for *The Fastest Gun Alive* by David Henry Wilson and Penguin Books Ltd. for *Green Smoke* by Rosemary Manning.

Illustrations by Leonora Box
Jon Davis
Maggie Ling

Oliver & Boyd
Robert Stevenson House
1–3 Baxter's Place
Leith Walk
Edinburgh EH1 3BB

A Division of Longman Group UK Ltd.

First published 1983
Third impression 1987

© Oliver & Boyd 1983

All rights reserved; no part of this book may be reproduced or transmitted, in any form or by any means electronic, mechanical, photocopying, recording or otherwise, without the prior written permission of the Publishers

ISBN 0 05 003377 8

Produced by Longman Group (FE) Ltd
Printed in Hong Kong

Contents

1 The Fastest Gun Alive
        Part 1: Pritchett's a Baddie   5
2 Alphabetical Order   7
3 The Fastest Gun Alive
        Part 2: Gunning for Pritchett   9
4 The Wild West
        Part 1: Where was the West?   14
5 Context Clues   16
6 The Wild West
        Part 2: The Cattle Towns (1860–1885)   19
7 The Wild West
        Part 3: Baddies and Goodies   22
8 Dictionary   29
9 The Wild West
        Part 4: The Fast Draw   31
10 Sequence   33
11 Jason The Hero   36
12 Finding Proof   39
13 The Shy Dragon   42
14 Dreaded Monster   45
15 Making Inferences   48
16 Little Robin Redbreast   51
17 Main Ideas   58
18 Christmas Customs   61
19 The Story Of Skiing   65
20 Details   67
21 Althetes On Skis   70

Preface

The materials in *Reading Well* are intended to assist pupils in the acquisition and development of higher order reading skills.

The authors have sought to include a wide range of writing for children of the relevant age group. Extracts from children's fiction are taken from a wide variety of writers. In making the selection regard was had to books which seemed to be popular in school and class libraries. Moreover, attempts have been made to select extracts which are interesting and might encourage pupils to read more of the books chosen. In all these extracts, quality was the major criterion for selection, but enjoyment played a strong part.

An almost equal amount of space has been given to non-fiction. Children need to consult such material as they read to learn. Such reading is particularly important in the field of environmental studies, and there is a deliberate attempt to focus on material which they may well use in this area of the curriculum.

The skills to be taught and/or developed are skimming, recognising the main idea in a paragraph, selecting details to support the main idea, summarising, following ideas or events in sequence, using context clues, distinguishing between fact and opinion, recognising cause and effect, and finding proof. For the convenience of teachers, the questions have been grouped under these headings.

Interspersed throughout the book are skills pages designed to help in the teaching of specific skills. Teachers may wish to use those pages in a sequence quite different from that found in the book, especially since each skill is used in units that appear before the teaching page and hence the teacher will wish to exercise discretion.

It would be quite unrealistic to try deliberately to focus on every higher reading skill in every passage. Some of the questions in "Understanding the Passage" sections might well have appeared under other headings, but the intention is to ensure general understanding and to direct special attention to a few skills in each unit.

Many of the questions will lend themselves to much discussion and interaction because of differing interpretations by the pupils. Discussion will often be preceded by the questions in oral form. On other occasions the teacher may wish the pupils to write their answers in advance of discussion. In very many cases there will be alternative and competing answers.

As a rough guide, the sequence of units is in accordance with the increasing order of difficulty of reading content.

John Cooper   George Livingstone

1 The Fastest Gun Alive

Part 1: Pritchett's a Baddie

Little Melvin Woolaway was very upset when he came home from school today. Mr Pritchett, the headmaster, had said that he was talking during prayer time. Even worse than that, Mr Pritchett ordered ten housepoints off because Melvin had talked. Poor little Melvin, he felt he was in disgrace with everyone else in his house at school. Big disgrace! Ten whole housepoints!

Melvin had been talking. But all he had done was to ask another boy to get off his foot. Melvin even said "please". He felt that the whole world was unfair. It was Melvin's worst ever day at Wimpleford Junior School.

His class teacher tried to comfort him. His mother made him a special tea. Nothing seemed to help, he was still miserable. Nothing, that is, until the western came on. "The Fastest Gun Alive" was its name. That made him feel a bit better.

But by the time he went to bed the miseries had come back again. Poor little Melvin. But finally, his eyes closed and his body went to sleep. His brain stayed awake, however, and it went off on its own path. As he slept, Melvin's brain took him off down the dusty trail to Wimpleford Creek, Wild West town . . . .

(From *The Fastest Gun Alive!* by David Henry Wilson)

Questions

Understanding the passage

1. What had happened to Melvin at school?
2. How did he feel about it?
3. Was he guilty? Why?
4. Who tried to help him?
5. What did help him?
6. What happened that night?
7. What do you think will happen next?

2 Alphabetical Order

In Book 1, Inspector I. N. Quire gave you these rules:

1. Know your alphabet well.
2. Look at the first letters of the words.
3. When words have the same first letter, look at the second letters of the words.

The Inspector has more here for you—especially about using a dictionary, an encyclopedia or a telephone directory.

Examples

1. When words begin with the same *two* letters, you have to look next at the third letters in the words.
   Sea, second, see, segment are in the correct order.

2. In a telephone directory, the same rule works.
   So, *Adams, Adcock, Addison, Adkins* are in the correct order.

3. In a telephone directory, what happens when people have the same last name? Then, the order is decided by putting their first names into alphabetical order.
   So, *Livingstone, Alec; Livingstone, Andrew; Livingstone, Arthur; Livingstone, David* are in the correct order.

4. In an encyclopedia, some words begin with capital letters. A capital letter makes no difference to the order.
   So, *Lazarus, lion, Livingstone, lizard,* are in the correct order.

Exercises

1. *Put these words into the correct order for a dictionary.*
   read   rest   red   reckon   reef   rebel   refer   regal

2. *Put these words into the correct alphabetical order.*
   love   lord   lost   lot   low   loud   loyal

3. *Two words are out of order in this list. Put the words into the correct order.*
   refer   regal   reheat   rekindle   reign   reload   rejoin

4. *Put these words into the correct order for an encyclopedia.*
   lion   Limerick   lizard   Lister   Lincoln   Liddell   light   lily

5. *Put these words into the correct alphabetical order.*
   sago   Samson   Sawyer   saddle   saint   Saxon   salmon   Saracen

6. *Put these names into the correct order for a telephone directory.*
   Heston   Henderson   Hepburn   Heath   Hemmings   Herald   Hewitt   Heggison

7. *Put these names into the correct alphabetical order.*
   Smith, Adam   Smith, Matthew   Smith, Frank
   Smith, Alan   Smith, George   Smith, Freda
   Smith, Ann   Smith, Geraldine

Inspector I. N. Quire's New Rules for Alphabetical Order

1. When words begin with the same two letters, look at the third letter.
2. In an encyclopedia, capital letters do not change the order.
3. In a telephone directory, when people have the same last name the order is decided by the first names.

3 The Fastest Gun Alive

Part 2: Gunning for Pritchett

"Howdy, partner," says the old-timer sprawled out on the veranda.

Big Mel doesn't say a word, but walks straight past, shoulders his way through the swing-doors, and surveys the saloon. The drinking stops. The card-playing stops. The piano-playing stops. Everything stops. The whole crowd turns as one man to gaze at the tall, powerful stranger.

The tall, powerful, two-gun stranger speaks:

"I'm lookin' fer Pritchett," he says.

Nobody moves. The bar-tender licks his lips nervously.

"He ... he ain't here, mister."

The tall, powerful, two-gun, lethal-with-either-hand stranger looks straight into the eyes of the bar-tender, who squirms like a maggot on the end of that steely gaze.

"Go git him," says the stranger.

"Yes, sir!" says the bar-tender.

9

"And tell him . . ." says the stranger ". . . tell him Big Mel sent yer."

The bar-tender scurries out like a mouse that's just bumped into a tiger. Big Mel walks slowly to the bar, and the crowd falls back to make way for him.

"Give us some o' that there apple-pie," says Big Mel, and a woman hurries to obey.

"Make that a double," says Big Mel.

"Here y'are, Big Mel," says the woman.

"Thanks, honey," says Big Mel. "What's yer name?"

"Belle," says the woman. "Belle Arnold."

"I likes custard wi' my apple-pie, Belle."

"Sure thing, Big Mel."

The crowd gaze on in disbelief as Big Mel crunches the apple-pie in his powerful jaws, and gulps down the custard as if it were weak as water.

"Now," says Big Mel, coldly scanning the crowd, "any of you folks friends o' Pritchett?"

Not a murmur.

"Cos if y'are," says Big Mel, with a ghost of a smile flickering over his handsome lips, "ye'd better start sayin' prayers for 'im. And I don't want no talkin' in them prayers either, or I'll be puttin' ten bullets through yer hide."

The bar-tender creeps through the door.

"He's comin', Big Mel. Pritchett's comin'. An' he's real sore. He's bin knockin' housepoints off everyone he sees."

"When I've finished with 'im," says Big Mel, "he'll be a lot sorer than he is now."

The saloon doors swing open, and there stands the dreaded Pritchett, seven feet tall with a face like a boiled beetroot. There's a mad scramble as everyone dives for cover—everyone, that is, except Big Mel Woolaway, who leans casually on the bar, licking the apple-pie crumbs off his lips.

"Stand up when I come into the room!" says Pritchett. "Five housepoints off!"

A murmur of horror goes round the saloon—rising up from under the tables where all the heads are hiding.

"Are you speakin' ter me?" says Big Mel.

"Don't answer back, boy," says Pritchett.

Big Mel slowly straightens up ... and up ... and up, until his head nearly touches the ceiling, and he gazes down on little Pritchett like a giraffe gazing down on a baby chimpanzee. "So you're Pritchett," he says. "You don't remember me."

"I certainly do not," says Pritchett, trembling a little.

"I'm Little Mel," says Big Mel. "Little Mel Woolaway. An' I've come for my housepoints."

"H ... h ... house-p ... p ... points?" says Pritchett.

"TEN!" roars Big Mel. "An' I wannem now."

"But ... but ... I haven't got any here," says Pritchett, beginning to look more like a cabbage than a beetroot.

"I wannem, Pritchett," says Big Mel. "An' if I don't gettem, I'm gonna fill you so full o' holes you'll look like a packet o' Polos."

With a desperate lunge, Pritchett reaches for his cane, but before he can raise it higher than his hip ... piaow! piaow! ... two shots, and he's left holding a splinter. There's a gasp from under the tables. The voice of Belle peals forth:

"Gee, he's the fastest gun alive!"

"Hold up that thar splinter," says Big Mel.

Pritchett's hand goes up, like a five-fingered jelly.

"Keep it still," says Big Mel, "if you don't want them hands turnin' into mittens."

Piaow! And the splinter goes flying.

"Now then, Pritchett," says Big Mel, "do I get my housepoints, or do I take your fingernails off?"

"You ... you ... you g ... g ... get your h ... h ...

housep ... p ... points," says Pritchett. "T ... t ... twenty!"

Two guns whirl like Catherine-wheels on Big Mel's fingers, and then he slides them back into their holsters.

"Go get 'em," he says.

"Y ... y ... y ..."

"Stop talkin', boy!" says Big Mel. "An' get goin'."

Pritchett backs out of the saloon like a whipped dog, bodies crawl out from under tables like worms after a shower, and Big Mel—Huge Mel—smiles the smile of a satisfied lion.

"Milk all round!" says Big Mel. "An' make mine a double."

(From *The Fastest Gun Alive!* by David Henry Wilson)

Questions

Understanding the passage

1. What happened when Big Mel entered the saloon? Why?
2. Who was Big Mel looking for?
3. How did the bar-tender behave? Why?
4. What did Big Mel order? How did the crowd behave?
5. What did Pritchett look like?
6. Why did everyone dive for cover?
7. What did Pritchett order Big Mel to do?
   What did Big Mel do in reply?
8. What did Big Mel demand?
   How did Pritchett behave?
9. What happened next?
10. Who won in the end? Why did Big Mel say, "Stop talkin' boy"?

Main ideas and details (See pages 58 to 60, and 67 to 69.)

Here are three of the main ideas in the passage.
(a) Big Mel is the big, fearless hero.
(b) Pritchett is the villain.
(c) Everybody else is weak.

In the passage there are many examples of details which support each of these three main ideas.
Read through the passage and make a list of the details which support each of the main ideas.
   You might write down your lists like this:

(a) *Big Mel (hero)*
   1. Tall and powerful
   2. —
   3. —
   4. etc.

(b) *Pritchett (villain)*
   1. Real sore
   2. —
   3. —
   4. etc.

(c) *Everybody else (weak)*
   1. Bar-tender squirms like a maggot
   2. —
   3. —
   4. etc.

4 The Wild West

Part 1: Where was the West?

The story called "The Fastest Gun Alive" was about the Wild West in America. The people in the story behaved just as they do in films and on TV. We have all seen lots of these adventures and we know from them what life was like in those times. We all know the names of "goodies" like Wild Bill Hickock, Wyatt Earp and Pat Garret. We know too of the "baddies" like Billy the Kid, Butch Cassidy, Jesse James and Belle Starr. Place names like Abilene and Dodge City we have all heard of time and again.

But were things really like they are in the films and on TV? Were the "goodies" good? Were the "baddies" bad? Were the sheriffs and marshalls really such great heroes? Were they all fast on the draw? Did they have shoot-outs where everybody behaved according to the rules? Was life really as glamorous as we are made to believe that it was?

Before we go on to look into these questions maybe we could just stop and get one or two things straight. Look at the map opposite and answer the questions.

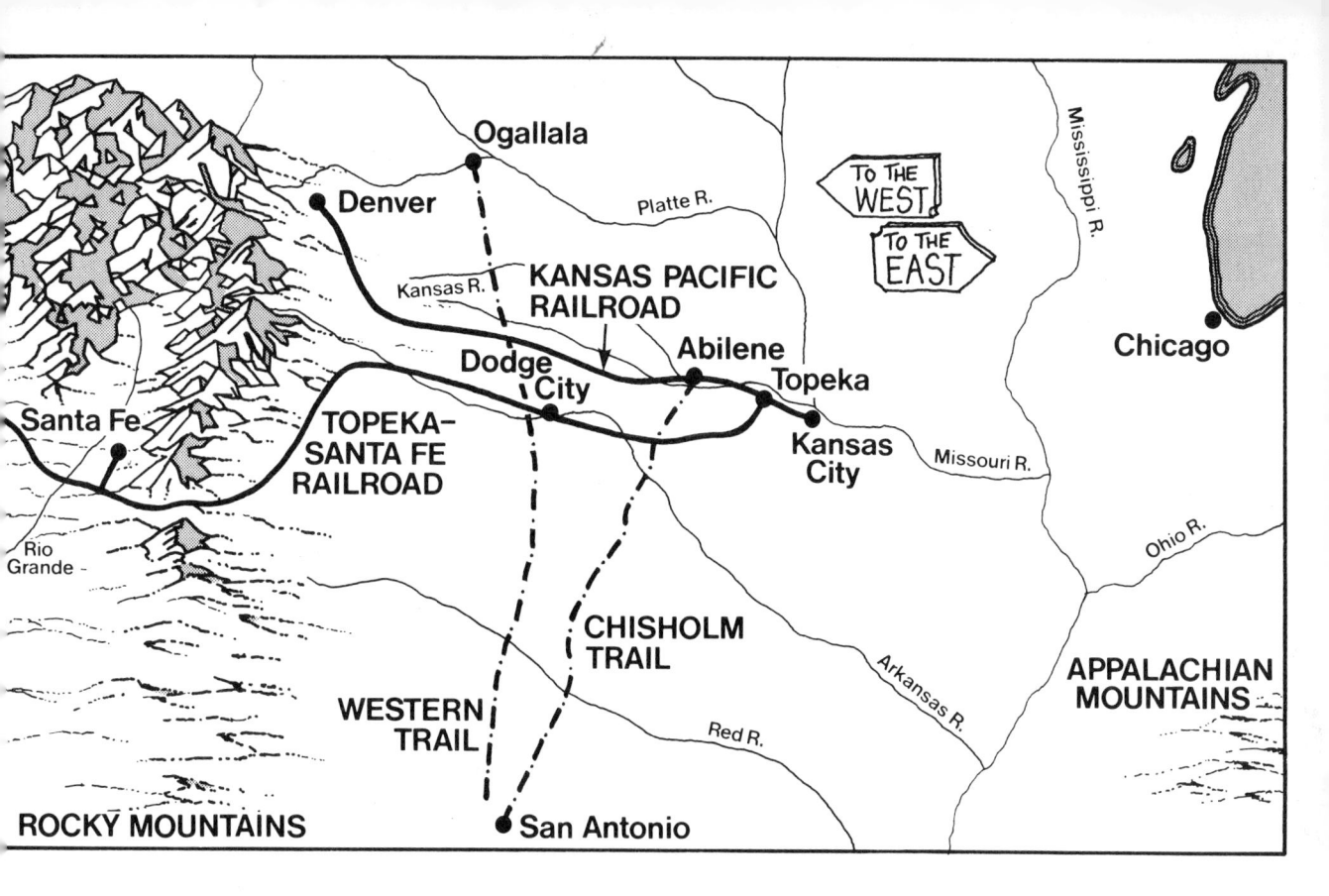

1. Find Abilene and Dodge. Are they in the West? Where would you say they are?
2. What runs through Abilene and Dodge?
3. Move east from Abilene. What big places do you come to?
4. What leads to Abilene and Dodge from the south?
5. Can you guess why Abilene and Dodge are joined to the other big towns?

Questions

Finding proof (See pages 39 to 41.)

Here are some statements about the passage.
Read each one and say whether you think that it is true *or* false.
Say why you think so.
(a) We all know all about the Wild West.
(b) Films and TV shows tell us what the West was really like.
(c) Maybe things in the West were not really as they are shown in films and on TV.
(d) The West was not in the least way like it is in films and on TV.

5 Context Clues

In Book 1, Inspector I. N. Quire gave you these rules:

1. If you don't know at all what a word means, look at the context for clues.
2. If you don't know which meaning a word has, look at the context for clues.
3. If you want to be sure, use your dictionary to check that you are right.

Remember that the context simply means the words near to the unknown word.

These rules do not change. But, like the cases the Inspector has to work on, the words and the clues can be more difficult.

Examples

1. The same word can have different meanings. It is important to choose the correct one. The correct meaning is the one which suits the word as it is used in the passage.
You must look at the context for clues to the correct meaning.
Here is a report which the Inspector was given. In the report the word *watch* is used four times. *Watch* has a different meaning each time.

The policeman had to *watch* the prisoners. He was worried because his *watch* was broken. He did not know how long it would be before the next policeman came on duty and his *watch* would end. All that he could do was to try to stay awake and *watch* the prisoners' every move.

Here are four meanings for the word *watch*. Below that the Inspector gives his meaning for each time *watch* was used. He also gives the clues which helped him to decide.

meanings
(a) a small clock worn on the wrist
(b) to look at carefully
(c) to guard
(d) a turn at guard duty

                                                  clues

1. means *to guard* (c)   "watch the prisoners" was the clue.

2. means *a small clock* (a)   "his watch was broken" was the clue.

3. means *a turn at guard duty* (d)   "the next policeman would come on duty" and "watch would end" were the clues.

4. means *to look at carefully* (b)   "watch the prisoners' every move" was the clue.

Can you see now how he worked out the meanings?

2. Inspector I. N. Quire was reading a story to his son. There were some words his son did not know the meaning of. Here is the story, the meanings of the words and the context clues the Inspector used to help his son.

Jack had to find some way out of the terrible *predicament*. The monster roared with fury. Fire shot from its nostrils. Its whole body shook with rage.

"Have a water biscuit," said Jack nervously.

"You *impertinent* pup!" roared the monster. "How dare you cheek me!"

The flames grew longer and hotter. Then suddenly the rage *diminished*, the shaking stopped.

"Got any custard creams?" *queried* the dragon, "I just love them."

	words	meanings	context clues
1.	predicament	*a dangerous situation*	Jack was in deep trouble with the angry monster.
2.	impertinent	*cheeky*	The monster thought Jack was trying to "cheek" it.
3.	diminished	*grew smaller or less*	The monster stopped being angry.
4.	queried	*asked*	The monster asked a question.

Exercises

1. *Check the meanings of these words in your dictionary to see if the Inspector was correct. Remember to put them into alphabetical order first.*

    predicament   impertinent   diminished   queried

2. *In each of these sentences one word is underlined. There is a list of meanings for the words, but the meanings are in the wrong order. Choose the correct meaning for each word.*

sentences	meanings
(a) The noise subsided.	doesn't work as it should
(b) The rickety ladder was unsafe.	cried out
(c) "Ouch!" she exclaimed.	lit
(d) The defective engine stopped.	a route, a plan for a journey
(e) The travellers planned their itinerary.	grew less, died away
(f) A lantern illuminated the door.	shaky, not safe

6 The Wild West

Part 2: The Cattle Towns (1860~1885)

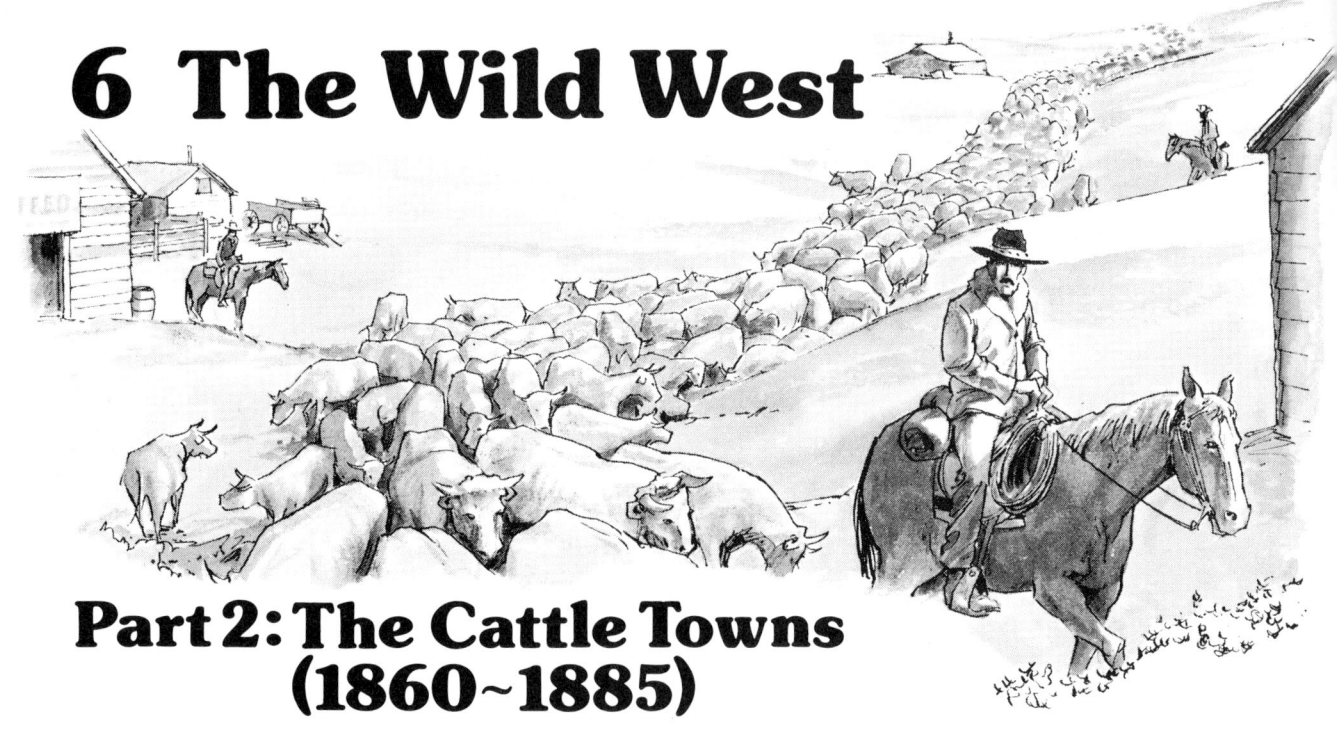

Abilene was the first of the big cattle towns. In 1860 it was just a dozen log huts. Then the Kansas Pacific Railroad arrived, and that was when Abilene began to grow.

In New York and Chicago there were thousands of people who needed more and more food. In Texas there were thousands of cattle which could provide food for these people. Once the railroad came to Abilene the Texans could drive the cattle up the Chisholm Trail for 1000 miles to Abilene. They sold the cattle in Abilene and then the cattle were put into railroad trucks and taken East to provide food. This trade soon grew and between 1867 and 1871 over a million and a half cattle were herded into Abilene. Soon afterwards the Kansas Pacific Railroad was built further west and a new cattle town took over from Abilene using the Western Trail.

The Topeka–Santa Fe Railroad was built later. On this railroad stood Dodge. Dodge City was the last cattle town and perhaps the most famous one. The Texans could use the Western Trail to herd their cattle to Dodge.

These cattle towns were wild places. They became bigger because of the railroads and the cattle trade. They were rich towns for the same reason that they were wild towns. The reason for both of these things was that when the cowboys reached the cattle town, they were paid. After months on the trail they had plenty of money to spend and they were ready for a wild time. They spent their money on clothes, food, hotels, drinking and gambling. They nearly all carried a gun. Often they had fights. But they did not kill each other off in gun fights as in the films. Dodge City was supposed to be the wildest cattle town, but even there there were only 15 killings between the years 1870–1885. Perhaps the cowboys were bad shots? Or too drunk to shoot straight? A man called Teddy Abbott travelled round the cattle towns and wrote down what he saw. This story tells of some of the wild things that the cowboys got up to.

Abbott went to watch a play one night. In one part of the play a man was beating his wife and the noise on the stage wakened up a cowboy who had been sleeping. "He gave one jump on to the stage and busted the fellow on the head with his six gun before he remembered where he was. The woman got up and began to yell at him, all hell broke loose, somebody pulled Bill off the stage, they called the law, the boys shot out the lights and everybody broke their necks getting away from there."

When the cattle stopped coming to Abilene and Dodge, so did the cowboys. When the cowboys stopped coming the towns were not so wild. Other people came to these towns and the towns settled down. These towns are the ones where the events in lots of western films are supposed to have taken place. What do you think now? Was the "West" wild? Why was it called wild?

Questions

Understanding the passage

1. Why did Abilene begin to grow?
2. Why was Abilene called a cattle town?
3. What did the big cities need? How did the railroad help?
4. Why did Abilene stop being so important?
5. What was special about Dodge City?
6. Why were the cattle towns so wild?
7. Were there really lots of killings in the cattle towns? How do you know?
8. How did Abilene and Dodge stop being so wild?

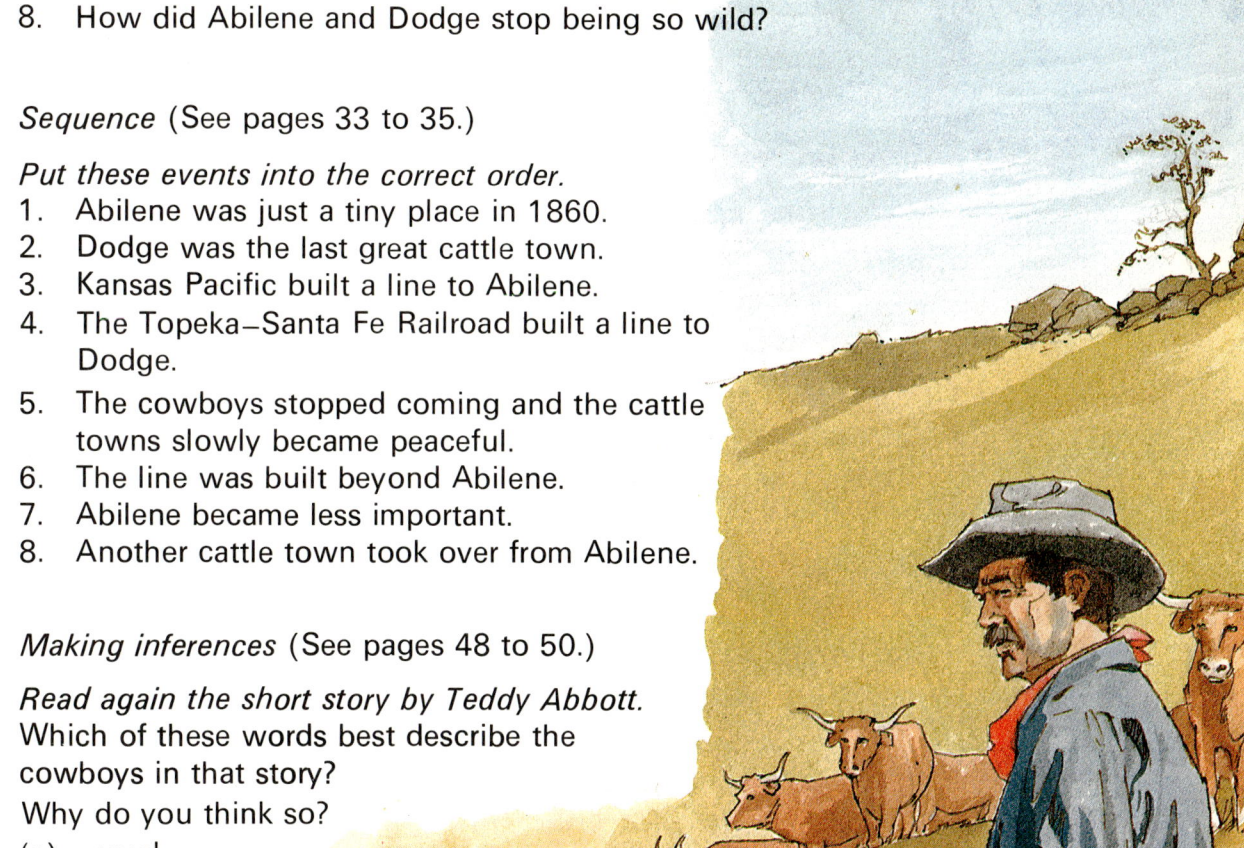

Sequence (See pages 33 to 35.)

Put these events into the correct order.
1. Abilene was just a tiny place in 1860.
2. Dodge was the last great cattle town.
3. Kansas Pacific built a line to Abilene.
4. The Topeka–Santa Fe Railroad built a line to Dodge.
5. The cowboys stopped coming and the cattle towns slowly became peaceful.
6. The line was built beyond Abilene.
7. Abilene became less important.
8. Another cattle town took over from Abilene.

Making inferences (See pages 48 to 50.)

Read again the short story by Teddy Abbott. Which of these words best describe the cowboys in that story? Why do you think so?
(a) cruel
(b) naughty
(c) wicked
(d) murderous
(e) wild
(f) fun-loving
(g) very funny
(h) ordinary

7 The Wild West

Part 3: Baddies and Goodies

By 1880, the law was beginning to cut down on the wild, lawless places. But it was a slow and gradual and difficult job to make these places lawful. So let's have a look at some of the baddies, some of the goodies, and how they really behaved.

A. The Baddies

Billy the Kid
Here are two verses from a song about William Bonney (alias Antrim, alias Wright) called Billy the Kid.

> When Billy the Kid was a very young lad
> In old Silver City he went to the bad,
> Way out in the West with a gun in his hand
> At the age of twelve years he killed his first man.
>
> Fair Mexican maidens play guitars and sing
> A song about Billy their boy bandit king,
> Now ere his young manhood had reached its sad end,
> He'd a notch in his pistol for twenty-one men.

In more than five hundred books Billy is made into a laughing, gentle young man who went to the bad because he lived among wild, bad people. They tell amazing stories of a boy who was good at cards at the age of eight and killed a man who insulted his mother at the age of twelve. He was a gay, laughing fellow who rode with other young desperadoes. He was bold, handsome, neatly dressed, very polite to young and old.

Looking at the facts and *not* the stories, what do we find? What do the history books say?

(a) Born in 1859 or 1860 in New York. Father died when he was young. Family moved to New Mexico. Billy went to school and took a job in a hotel when his mother died.

(b) In 1875, he was arrested for stealing clothes. He escaped. He next turned up at Camp Grant, Arizona where he murdered "Windy" Cahill who was beating him in a fight. He stole a horse and fled.

(c) In 1877, he was working as a cowboy in his old territory, New Mexico. His boss was involved in a fight with other businessmen. Both sides had gangs. Billy's boss was murdered and in return Billy shot Sheriff William Brady and his deputy. He fled again and took to cattle and horse stealing.

(d) A price of 1 500 dollars was put on his head. This was later increased to 5 000 dollars. In 1880, Pat Garret was appointed sheriff of Lincoln County, New Mexico to catch Billy. For months he followed Billy and finally captured him.

(e) In March 1881, Billy was sentenced to death. On 28th April he escaped by killing two deputies. Pat Garret set off after him and two months later he traced him to a house in Fort Sumner. Garret shot him dead just after midnight.

Here is the last verse of the song you read before.

> Now this is how Billy met his fate,
> The bright moon was shining, the hour was late,
> Shot down by Pat Garret who once was his friend,
> The young outlaw's life had now come to an end.

Billy did seem to laugh a lot. Pat Garret said "Those who know him well will tell you that in his most dangerous moods his face always wore a smile. He ate and laughed, drank and laughed, talked and laughed, rode and laughed—and killed and laughed."

Questions

Main ideas and details
(See pages 58 to 60 and 67 to 69.)

Complete these sentences to make main ideas.
(a) In the song and stories Billy was . . . .
(b) In the history books Billy was . . . .

Now pick out the details from the passage which support your two ideas.

You might make two lists like these:

Song and stories
1. Killed first man when 12
2. etc.

History books
1. When 15 stole clothes and ran away from jail.
2. etc.

Making inferences (See pages 48 to 50.)
1. Why do you think the song and the stories described Billy as they did?
2. Pat Garret agreed that Billy laughed a lot. What do you think he meant when he said those things about Billy?

B. **The Goodies**

1. *Wild Bill Hickock*
1. James Butler Hickock got the name "Wild Bill" not only because he was famous as a gun man but also because he had been involved in a lot of illegal doings before, during and after the American Civil War (1861–65). He was tried for murder and found not guilty.
2. In 1871, Wild Bill was made marshal of Abilene. He was only the second marshal. The first was Tom Smith who was murdered. Hickock was not a very good marshal. He spent his time drinking and gambling instead of patrolling the streets. His reputation as a gunman protected him. He shot and killed two men in a fight. One of them was his own deputy whom he shot by mistake.
3. After a year he was sacked. He drifted on to do lots of other jobs. He appeared in Buffalo Bill's Wild West Show.
4. In 1876, when he was old and going blind, he was shot in the back by a gunman in a saloon in Deadwood, Dakota.

5. Tom Smith, the first marshal of Abilene was a better marshal than Hickock. Before he took over, the Mayor of Abilene had made a rule that no guns were to be carried in the town. The notice was soon shot full of holes. Smith tried to make the cowboys obey the rule. One cowboy refused and Smith hit him and took his gun away. Another one did the same, so Smith took his gun, hit him on the head with it and ordered him out of town. Smith did not have much bother after that. He patrolled the streets regularly looking for trouble. He was shot dead by two farmers when he went to arrest them in November 1870.

6. If he was so good, I wonder why we never hear much about Tom Smith?

Questions

Understanding the passage

1. How did Hickock get his name?
2. What kind of man was he?
3. Was he good at his job as marshal? How do you know?
4. How did he die?
5. Who was Tom Smith?
6. What kind of man was he?
7. Was he good at his job? How do you know?
8. How did he die?

Making inferences (See pages 48 to 50.)

1. Why do you think Hickock became famous, but Smith did not? Can you suggest any reasons for that?
2. Do you think that Hickock deserved to be famous? Why?

Alphabetical order, context clues, dictionary (See pages 29 to 30.)

1. Here is a list of the meanings of some of the words in the passage.
   Find a word in the passage for each meaning. The number tells you the paragraph in which you will find the word.
   (a) drawn into, a part of (1)
   (b) against the law (1)
   (c) moving around and watching for trouble (2)
   (d) fame, name (2)
   (e) stopped him being harmed (2)
   (f) wandered along with no aim or purpose (3)
   (g) moved around and watched for trouble (5)
   (h) often (5)

   Now put your words into the correct alphabetical order. Then check your answers by using your dictionary.

2. *Wyatt Earp*

Wyatt Earp is probably the most famous lawman in the West. Like a lot of other famous men and women in the West, lots of cheap stories were written about him — in the East.

At one time he was a policeman in Wichita and later he became assistant marshal in Dodge City. The most famous gunfight in the West must be the gunfight at the OK Corral. In it, Wyatt, his two brothers Virgil and Morgan, and a gambler called Doc Holliday were supposed to have killed five outlaws in the space of a minute. The other three were wounded in the gunfight, but not Wyatt. Wyatt died peacefully in bed in 1929.

It is uncertain whether any of the events at the OK Corral really happened. Wyatt was tall and handsome and he did have brothers called Virgil and Morgan. In the 1880s in Dodge City there was trouble between two groups who were both trying to run the town council. Today we would vote about these things, but not then. There was a lot of bitterness between the two sides and Wyatt, Bat Masterton and other gunmen supported one of the sides. However, although the newspapers said there was bound to be trouble, the two sides settled the quarrel without bloodshed.

So why did Wyatt Earp become so famous?

Questions

Understanding the passage

1. Why was Earp so famous?
2. Where did he hold posts as a lawman?
3. What was supposed to have happened at the gunfight at the OK Corral?
4. What probably did actually happen?
5. How did Earp die?

Finding proof (See pages 39 to 41.)

1. Here are some statements.
   Read each one and decide whether it is true *or* false, *or whether the passage* doesn't say. *Say why you think so.*
   (a) The gunfight at the OK Corral never happened.
   (b) The gunfight at the OK Corral did happen.
   (c) The gunfight at the OK Corral may have happened.
   (d) The gunfight at the OK Corral probably did not happen.
   (e) The gunfight at the OK Corral probably did happen.
   (f) The gunfight at the OK Corral was just made up by story-writers.

8 Dictionary

In Book 1, Inspector I. N. Quire gave you these rules:

1. Practise your alphabetical order.
2. If you have a lot of words to look up, put them into alphabetical order before you begin.
3. Make sure that you choose the best meaning when you look up a word. To do that, you must look at the context for clues.

These rules do not change. But, like the cases the Inspector has to work on, the work can become more difficult.

Examples

1. Here is a list of words from a dictionary. They are in the correct order.

    face   fair   fancy   fast   film   fine

2. Now for some detective work.
   Here are some meanings for two of these words. Which words?

	meanings	words
(a)	blonde; just and honest; halfway between good and poor; not raining.	fair (fair can have all of these meanings)

	meanings	words
(b)	stuck, not able to move; a time without food; at great speed	fast (fast can have all of these meanings)

3. Here are some meanings for two more of the words. Which words? This time one part of each meaning is wrong. Which part?

	words	meanings	wrong
(a)	face	to turn towards; the front part of the head; part of a clock which shows the time; *part of a sequence.*	"part of a sequence" The word for that is "phase".

	words	meanings	wrong
(b)	fine	*discover;* when the weather is good; money paid as a punishment in court.	"discover" The word for that is "find".

Exercises

1. *Here is a list of words from a dictionary. Put them into the correct alphabetical order.*

    stand   spring   stone   sneak   strike   sole   soft   step   state

2. *Here are some meanings for four of these words. Which words?*
    (a) to move secretly; to betray someone; a person who can't be trusted.
    (b) to jump through the air; where water appears from underground; a metal coil; one of the seasons.
    (c) a precious jewel; an old measure of weight; a piece of rock; a hard seed in fruit.
    (d) gentle or mild; not hard; quiet, not loud.
    Use your dictionary to check your answers.
    Remember you have already put the words in alphabetical order.

3. *Here are some meanings for three more of the words. Which words? One part of each meaning is wrong. Which part? Say what word suits that wrong part.*
    (a) the only one; a flat fish; the bottom of a shoe; the spirit of a dead person.
    (b) to be upright on your feet; bitten by an insect; part of a sportsground with seats; a platform on which to show things.

Remember that the words are already in alphabetical order.
Now use your dictionary to check your answers.

9 The Wild West

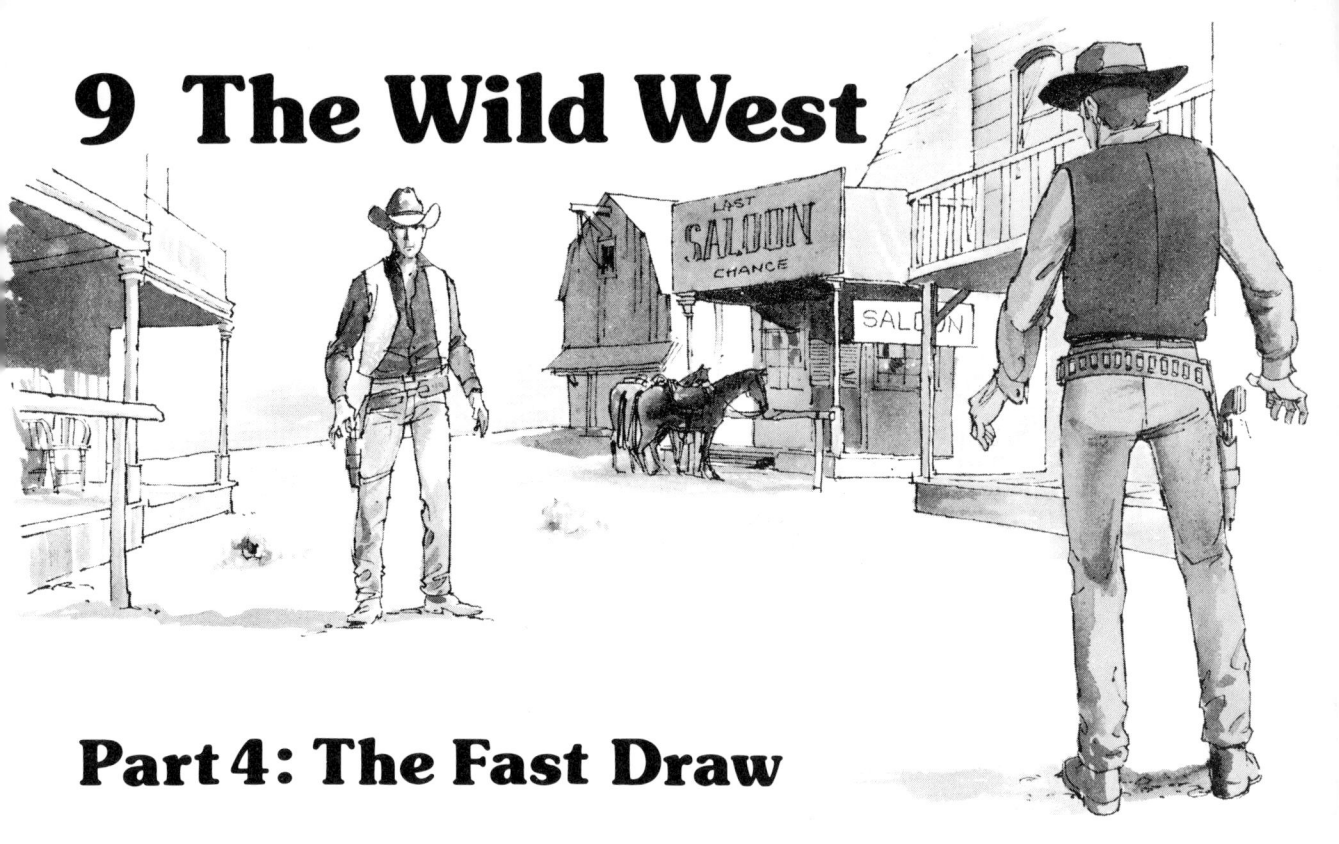

Part 4: The Fast Draw

You will have seen hundreds of times on the screen how the goodie or baddie had to be fast on the draw—get his gun out of its holster first. But was the fast draw really used in the old West?

First of all, you have to remember that the early revolvers were not easy to reload and use. Jesse James was a good shot, but being fast on the draw was something he knew nothing about. Secondly, the metal cartridge did not become common until well into the 1870s (Jesse was murdered in 1882).

Once these inventions came about, then being fast on the draw was possible. One way of helping the fast draw was to wear a cut-away holster. This meant that the butt of the gun and the trigger could be got hold of more quickly.

However fast a man could draw his gun, what really mattered was how well he could shoot. It was no good drawing first and then missing. And in any case, those "go for your guns" shoot outs you see on the screen did not really happen anyway. The professional gunman had to make sure he won. He had his gun out of its holster before the shooting was ready to start. He would also stoop to all sorts of tricks to make sure he was ready before his opponent.

The rules that you see the gunmen "play the game" by on the screen did not really happen either. They were too worried about shooting the other man in whatever way they could to bother about whether his gun was still in its holster, whether he had his back turned or whether he had a gun at all.

Questions

Understanding the passage

1. What happens often on the screen?
2. What question is asked about that?
3. What were the problems with early revolvers?
4. What was most important in a gunfight?
5. What was good about the cut-away holster?
6. How does a gunfight usually happen on the screen?
7. What happened in real gunfights? Why?
8. Was fair play important? Why?

Alphabetical order, context clues, dictionary

Here are two lists. One is a list of words from the passage. The other is a list of meanings for those words *as they are used in the passage*. The meanings are in the wrong order.

Match each word with its proper meaning. Two of the meanings are wrong for the words as they are used in the passage. Pick them out and make up your own meanings for them.

common	to hit with the head
butt	enemy
professional	a piece of land used for animals
opponent	earning his living in that way

Now put the words into alphabetical order and then check your answers in your dictionary.

10 Sequence

In Book 1, Inspector I. N. Quire gave you these rules:
1. Look at all the events carefully.
2. Decide which event happened first.
3. Decide which event happened last.
4. Put the other events in order.

These rules do not change, but, like the cases the Inspector works on, some examples are harder than others.

Examples

Here is a case which the Inspector worked on. Other policemen worked on the case first. They all handed their information on to the Inspector. When he got the information, it was all jumbled up. He had to sort out the correct sequence.

	Information	*Inspector's sequence*
(a)	The green car was found parked in the next town just after teatime that day.	7
(b)	Just after half-past three, a green car raced off down the High Street.	5
(c)	At 2 pm a green car was reported stolen from the centre Car Park.	1
(d)	The robbers made off with a load of diamond rings.	4
(e)	Someone noticed some men sitting in a green car round the corner from High Street.	2
(f)	The robbery was reported to the police at 3.35 pm.	6
(g)	At 3.30 pm three masked men burst into the jewellers in High Street.	3

Here are his notes of the correct sequence.
1. Green car reported stolen at 2 pm.
2. Green car with men in it seen near jewellers.
3. 3.30 pm men enter shop.
4. Men steal diamonds.
5. Men race off in stolen car.
6. Police learn of robbery at 3.35 pm.
7. Stolen car found later in next town.

Exercises

1. *What is wrong in these statements?*
   Mary said, "We'll meet in front of the cinema at 5 pm exactly. Don't be late! I don't like waiting outside. So, if you're not there, I'll just go on in and I'll see you inside."
   "But how will I know if you are inside, or if you are late?" asked Jean.
   "I know what we'll do," said Mary. "If I'm there first, I'll chalk a mark on the wall. If you're there first, you can rub it off."

2. *Is there anything wrong with this statement?*
   The policeman asked the boy, "Were you on the lorry when you fell off?"

3. *Read these sentences. Then put them into the correct sequence.*
   (a) John cycled down to the shop and got what his mother wanted.
   (b) John went to get his bike.
   (c) John's mother asked him to go to the shop for her.
   (d) John went to see Tom and borrowed Tom's bicycle.
   (e) When he came out of the shop, the bicycle had gone.
   (f) John found that his bicycle had a puncture in the back tyre.

11 Jason The Hero

Jason, the prince, was looking for the Golden Fleece. If he could bring the Golden Fleece back to Iolchus, he could become king. After a long voyage and many terrible adventures, Jason and his men arrived at the city of Colchis near to where the Golden Fleece was.

Jason told the king why they had come. "I will give you the Golden Fleece if you can harness my bulls which breathe fire, plough a field with them and sow it with dragons' teeth," said the king.

Jason agreed at once. That night he sat wondering how he could possibly carry out this task. As he sat there, a woman came to speak to him. She was Medea, the king's daughter, and she was a witch. She told Jason that she could tell him how to do it. But in return he would have to take her with him and marry her. Jason agreed.

Medea gave him a magic ointment which would stop him from being wounded or burned by the bulls. He put the ointment on next morning and amazed everyone by easily putting a harness on the bulls. He ploughed the field and sowed it with dragons' teeth. That was when the next nasty shock happened.

The dragons' teeth began to grow at once. They grew into armed men ready to kill Jason. But Medea had warned him about this too. He flung his helmet into the midst of them and they at once fought and killed one another.

The king was furious but he had to keep the bargain. "Tomorrow you can have the Fleece," he said. But secretly he planned to murder Jason and his men and burn the *Argo*.

Again Medea warned him and in the night she led him to the place where the Fleece was hanging. It was guarded by an enormous dragon but Medea had a plan for that too. First she helped Orpheus, a wonderful musician, to sing a spell to put the dragon to sleep. Then she cast her magic again and the moon was darkened.

Jason climbed up the body of the sleeping dragon and unhooked the Fleece from its tree. By the light of the Fleece they hurried back to the *Argo* and set sail at once.

As they rowed away, the dragon wakened up and set up such a racket that all the people of Colchis were roused from their sleep. The king set off after them in a very fast ship.

Soon the king's ship caught up with them. Then Medea did a terrible thing. She had brought her brother on the *Argo* with her and now she grabbed him and killed him. Then she cut up his body in pieces and threw the pieces over the side. She knew that her father would stop to pick up the pieces from the sea. He did and the *Argo* got away.

Jason was as horrified as the rest of his men. There was nothing that he could do. She had helped him and he had to keep his promise. Not only had he to take her with him, he had to marry her.

Medea made him very unhappy and she did some other really awful things. In the end Jason died a lonely, unhappy old man. He was killed as he slept alone in the *Argo* many years later. The rotten front of the old ship fell on him and killed him.

(After the story of Jason as told in *Tales of the Greek Heroes* by Roger Lancelyn Green)

Questions

Understanding the passage

1. Where was the Fleece?
2. What task did the king of Colchis set Jason?
3. Who was Medea? How did she first help Jason? What did Jason have to do for her?
4. "The next nasty shock happened." What was the "nasty shock"? How did Jason manage?
5. How did Medea help Jason next?
6. Who was Orpheus? How did he help Jason?
7. What wakened the people of Colchis? What did they do?
8. How did Medea help Jason again? What did Jason think of her help?
9. What happened to Jason in the end?

Main ideas and details (See pages 58 to 60, and 67 to 69.)

1. Medea helped Jason in many ways. That is *one main idea* from the passage.
   Make a list of all the things (details) she did to help Jason. Number each part of your list.
2. Jason was a brave man who kept his promises. That is *another main idea* from the passage.
   Make a list of the events in the passage which are examples (details) to support that main idea.

12 Finding Proof

In Book 1, Inspector I. N. Quire gave you these rules:

1. Look carefully at the facts before you decide. Be sure about your evidence.
2. Never leap before you look.
3. There are three possible answers:
   True (proved) because there is enough evidence.
   False (wrong) because the evidence says the opposite.
   Not Proved because there is not enough evidence to prove that something is true or false.

Before you go on, the Inspector wants you to remember that what is important is the amount of evidence. Also, instead of using *Not Proved* we will use the phrase *doesn't say*. Doesn't say means the same as *Not Proved* and it is a short way of writing *the passage did not say that*.

Examples

Here is a short passage. At the end of it are some statements. We sent these to the Inspector to give us his expert opinion and to say why he thought that way.

Willow was a very different place from Granddad's old home in the South. He missed the green fields, the trees and his big garden. He missed his gardening most of all. Granddad had never taken to the high, bare slopes and the snow-filled valleys and the stony ground around Willow.

	statements:	opinion	reasons
(a)	Granddad used to be a keen gardener.	True	He missed gardening most of all.
(b)	Granddad had no garden in Willow.	Doesn't say	The passage only says he missed his big garden. Perhaps he had a smaller one.
(c)	Granddad was fond of the scenery where he lived now.	False	He had never taken to the new scenery.
(d)	Granddad now lived in a hilly place.	True	There are "high, bare slopes" and "snow-filled valleys".
(e)	Granddad was very unhappy in Willow.	Doesn't say	The passage only says that he was not as happy as he used to be.

Exercises

1. *Read this passage carefully. Then read the statements at the end. Which statements are* true, *which are* false, *for which would you decide the passage* doesn't say? *Say why you think so.*

   The Varmint Boys were outlaws. They were a real mean pair. No trick was too low for them. They kicked the table over if they were losing at Ludo. They stole washing off the line. It didn't matter if the clothes didn't fit them, they did it out of pure meanness. Calling people names was another of their skunky tricks. Folks were real glad to see the Varmints locked up.

   (a) The Varmints were awful crooks.
   (b) The Varmints were caught.
   (c) The Varmints were more naughty than they were wicked.
   (d) There were three Varmints.
   (e) People felt sorry for the Varmints.

2. *Read this passage carefully. Then read the statements at the end. Are the statements* true, false, *or do you think the passage* doesn't say? *Why do you think so?*

The girls thought that their brothers had all the fun. The boys fished, rode their bikes, played cricket, were noisy and got very dirty. They ate everything on the table and in the larder. On the other hand, the girls were expected to behave like perfect little ladies. Mother was very keen on that. They had to help with housework and cook. They never got any fun, they said.

(a) The boys were very badly behaved.
(b) The girls envied their brothers.
(c) The boys did not like the girls.
(d) Mother was cruel to the girls.
(e) Mother let the boys do just what they liked.

3. *Here is another passage. Do the same with it and with the statements as you did with the last two passages.*

The Gang had found a grand place to meet. There was a row of empty houses in the next street. The fourth house down had no lock on the back door. They sneaked in. There were four rooms in the house. In one room there were two big armchairs, a fireplace and curtains at the windows. There was even running water. The boys were delighted.

(a) The gang had permission to use the house.
(b) There was a chair for every member of the gang.
(c) The fireplace was running with water.
(d) Only one house had no lock on the back door.
(e) There were no girls in the gang.

13 The Shy Dragon

(Susan is on holiday with her mother in Cornwall, England. One day when she is walking along the beach on her own she is very surprised indeed. She sees smoke and hears a voice calling her from a cave. She finds that the owner of the voice claims to be a dragon. She does not believe him. Well, would you?)

Susan was not quite sure that she believed that whoever it was could be a dragon. Its voice sounded so undragonlike.

"Are you really a dragon?" she asked.

"Shall I come and show you?"

"Yes," said Susan bravely.

"Is there anyone else about? Shan't come if there is. Some people are so nasty about dragons."

"I'm not," said Susan. "I'm longing to see you, and there's no one else here, so do come out."

She had to screw up her courage to say this, because, after all, dragons can be rather alarming creatures. But Sue was stuffed full of curiosity, and she couldn't bear to go back till she had made sure whether the voice belonged to a real dragon or not. She was used to grown-ups pretending to be things that they are not.

Out of the cave came a green, scaly foot, well furnished with claws. Sue stepped back a little. It was safer to be near the rocks, she thought. Another foot appeared, and above it a large head, long like a horse's head, but bright green in colour and shining like glass. The creature had two ears and a pair of golden-yellow horns, very highly polished. His eyes were large and yellow too, like gleaming lamps. He did not look at all frightening. He seemed to have no teeth, and his wide, wide mouth was set in a charming smile.

"Shall I come out any further?" he asked.

"Well," began Sue, and hesitated.

"I promise I won't eat you," said the dragon. "I never eat anyone nowadays. I've quite changed my habits."

"Well," said Susan again. "I'd love to see your tail. Have you got a long one?"

The dragon turned slowly round, and Susan could see his scaly back, along the top of which were rows of yellow fins, rather like a fish's, only much bigger, and then he slowly uncoiled several yards of emerald green tail, decorated with yellow scales arranged in patterns. Laid close against his back, tidily folded, were his wings, which, like his tail, were green and scaly, and patterned with gold.

"Now are you sure I'm a dragon?" he said, and his voice sounded impatient.

"Oh, yes," said Susan. "I'm quite sure now. You couldn't be anything else."

Suddenly she remembered her mother. She knew she ought to be getting back, but she didn't want to hurt the dragon's feelings. He seemed so eager to talk to her. So she said, as politely as she knew how:

"Would you mind very much if I went back now?"

"I should mind," he answered at once. "You're such a nice little girl. So different from the silly creatures that run away from me screaming."

"Why do they scream?" asked Sue with interest, forgetting about her mother for the moment.

"They think I'm going to eat them."

"Well, you do eat people, in stories," said Sue.

"Oh, stories!" said the dragon scornfully. "Stories in your human books, I suppose, written by people who never saw a dragon in their lives."

(From *Green Smoke* by Rosemary Manning)

Questions

Sequence

Put these statements into the same order in which they happened in the story.
1. Susan did not believe she was listening to a dragon.
2. The dragon came completely out of the cave.
3. Susan remembered that she should get back to her mother.
4. Susan asked the dragon to come out of the cave.
5. The dragon promised that it had stopped eating people.

Finding proof

1. Which of these adjectives are *true* about Susan? Why do you think so? (More than one are true.)
    (a) brave (c) curious (e) cheeky
    (b) nosy   (d) foolish (f) cautious

2. Which of these statements are *true*? Why?
    (a) This was a gentle dragon who had never eaten people.
    (b) The dragon was cunning and was really going to eat Susan.
    (c) The dragon used to eat people but he really had stopped doing it.
    (d) The dragon enjoyed frightening people and that was why he lived in a cave.
    (e) The dragon lived in a cave because he was shy.

14 Dreaded Monster

1. There are many very old stories of dragons and these stories come from many parts of the world. In most of the stories the dragons are fierce, ugly, wicked creatures. But dragons are not the same the world over. When we look at dragons in stories from Europe we find that they are different from the dragons in stories from places such as China.

2. In Europe, dragons were like big, heavy snakes which had wings, legs and claws. Their wings pointed upwards, not outwards like a bird's wings. Although they could stretch their wings, they hardly ever flew in any of the stories. Dragons had all sorts of different colours and some were just plain black. The three things which all of these dragons had in common were that they always breathed fire and smoke, they were the enemies of man and they were terrifying, dangerous, ugly creatures.

3. In European stories, dragons lived in dark places far away from people. They lived in caves, or inside

mountains or even under water. Dragons were very rich but they were also very mean and greedy. They hid their gold and jewels underground or on the bottom of waters. They were so miserly that they would fight to the death any man who tried to steal any of their treasure.

4. In the East, dragons were different. There is an ancient Chinese dictionary which is 3500 years old and which gives a detailed description of an Eastern dragon. It had a head like a camel, ears like a bull, a neck like a snake, a belly like a frog and scales like a fish. Its claws were like an eagle's talons and its paws were like those of a tiger. It had 81 scales arranged in 9 rows of 9 (magic number) and its voice sounded like a banging gong. There were whiskers round its chin and a pearl under its chin. This pearl was where the dragon got its power from and if a man could steal the pearl then the dragon was helpless. This dragon had no wings but it had magic power which allowed it to soar into the air when it wanted to.

5. The Chinese believed that every sea, lake and river had a dragon living there. The dragons controlled the weather. Lightning happened when a dragon flashed its eyes. The wind was its breath. A storm happened when a dragon tore angrily at the water with its claws. These dragons could also make themselves invisible.

6. The Chinese also believed that dragons ran the world. There was the Heavenly Dragon which carried the palaces of the gods on its back. The Divine Dragon made it rain and the Earthly Dragon looked after streams and rivers. Finally, the Underground Dragon guarded the treasures which men were not allowed to have.

7. Even today the Chinese carry a paper dragon at the head of any parade on an important occasion. If

that sounds daft to you, just remember that some of our customs must seem just as daft to the Chinese. Anyway, better a paper dragon than a real one, I would think.

Questions

Finding proof

Which of these statements are *true?* Which one are *false?*
- (a) Chinese dragons were totally different from European dragons.
- (b) Chinese dragons were kind and European dragons were mean.
- (c) European and Chinese dragons were both like snakes in some way.
- (d) European dragons had claws, Chinese dragons had no claws.
- (e) Only European dragons breathed fire.
- (f) Chinese dragons were more important to the people than European dragons were.
- (g) Both European and Chinese dragons could live in water.

Main ideas and details (See pages 58 to 60, and 67 to 69.)

Here are some possible main ideas for the first two paragraphs. Which is the best one for each paragraph? Why?

Paragraph 1
- (a) Dragons were fierce, ugly, wicked creatures.
- (b) Dragon stories are common and widespread.
- (c) Dragons in Europe were different from those in China.

Paragraph 2
- (a) Dragons in Europe had different colours.
- (b) Dragons in Europe were the enemies of men.
- (c) Dragons in Europe differ in detail, but have important factors in common.

15 Making Inferences

In Book 1, Inspector I. N. Quire gave you these rules:

1. First of all, ask yourself, "What do I know?"
2. Remember what you know and then be ready to make a clever guess. Do not make a wild guess.
3. Always be ready to say why you made your inference.
4. Other people might make a different inference. Think about whether their inferences are *true* or *false*. (How much evidence is there?)

Before we go on, the Inspector has one or two more points to make to you.

1. Remember that you must make an intelligent guess or deduction.
2. Making inferences is quite like deciding it doesn't say in Finding Proof. When you have to make an inference it is because the evidence in the passage doesn't quite prove the statement.
3. Some of your evidence will be in the passage when you make an inference. But some of your evidence will also come from something that you knew before you read the passage.

Examples

Here is a short passage. We made some inferences and sent them to the Inspector to get his expert opinion. He told us whether he thought the inferences were *true* or *false*. He also told us why he thought so.

It was a wonderful June day. The kind of day when it's good to be alive. The frogs were singing in their deep-voiced way. The young otters were sliding down the bank into the river. The goose was watching over them like a life-guard. Even the snakes were contented as they lay asleep in the heat of the sun.

	inferences	opinion	evidence
(a)	the events happened in a zoo.	false	In a zoo these animals would not be kept together. Also there is a river in the passage.
(b)	it is a hot, sunny day.	true	June and "the heat of the sun".
(c)	it is more difficult to make a snake contented.	true	"even the snakes were contented".

We asked the Inspector why he thought that inference (a) was false. "After all," we said, "it doesn't say anything in the passage about where animals are kept." Here is his answer.

"I agree that it doesn't say anything about that in the passage, but that is something I knew before I read the passage. Sometimes when you make an inference you have to use the things that you know, as well as what it says in the passage."

Exercises

1. Here is a short passage. What inference can you make about Uncle Bill? *Say why you think so.*

Uncle Bill's house was full of interesting things brought from all over the world. Stools made from elephants' feet, cowboys' hats, Eskimos' boots and a rajah's turban. There was also a room full of glass cases with moths and insects on display.

2. *Read this passage.* What inference can you make about what the girls were going to do? *Say why you think so.*

They squealed with excitement.
"Maybe we'll see sea serpents," said Lucy.
"And desert islands and cannibals," said Agnes.
"And mermaids, and palm trees and sharks," said Elma.

3. *Read this passage.* What inferences can you make? Why do you think so?

He was a very strange-looking fox. He was grey and twice the size of most red foxes. He had only one eye and the other eye was all swollen and bruised. Part of one ear was missing and he had bare patches all over his coat. His coat was covered in mud and thorns and he was bleeding from several cuts.

Inspector I. N. Quire's New Rule for Making Inferences

There does usually have to be some evidence in the passage. But don't just depend on the evidence which is there. What you know will help you too.

16 Little Robin Redbreast

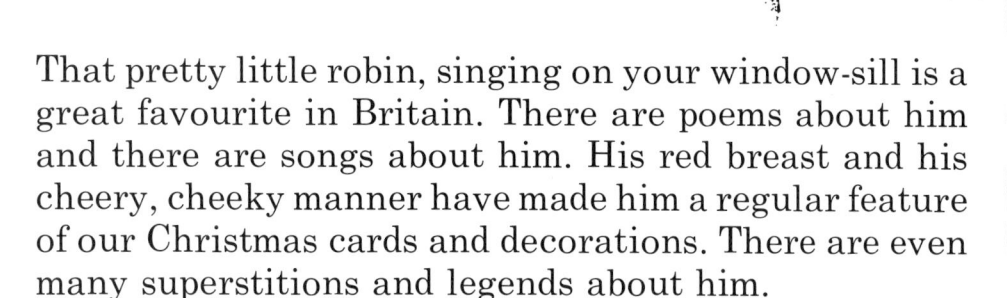

That pretty little robin, singing on your window-sill is a great favourite in Britain. There are poems about him and there are songs about him. His red breast and his cheery, cheeky manner have made him a regular feature of our Christmas cards and decorations. There are even many superstitions and legends about him.

It is easy to understand why he is so popular. His colour makes him stand out at a time of year when everything is grey and colourless. When other birds leave us for warmer places, he stays on with us through the cold, dark days of winter. It is his song that we hear. And he is so friendly! He will even come into the kitchen in search of crumbs.

No wonder we love him so much! He is such a cheerful, cheeky little chap. He is our friend who reminds us that colour will come back to our world when spring comes again.

* * * * *

In the next few pages you will find a poem about the friendly robin, some of the superstitions and legends about him, and some facts about him as a real bird. You may find it interesting to compare the facts with the robin in the poem, superstition and legend.

January

Cold the day and cold the drifted snow,
Dim the day until the cold dark night.
Crackle, sparkle, faggot; embers glow:
Some one may be plodding through the snow
Longing for a light.
For the light that you and I can show.
If no one else should come,
Here Robin Redbreast's welcome to a crumb,
And never troublesome:
Robin, why don't you come and fetch your crumb?

Here's butter for my hunch of bread,
And sugar for your crumb;
Here's room upon the hearthrug,
If you'll only come.

In your scarlet waistcoat,
With your keen bright eye,
Where are you loitering?
Wings were made to fly!

Make haste to breakfast,
Come and fetch your crumb,
For I'm as glad to see you
As you are glad to come.

Christina Rossetti

Questions

Read the poem.

1. *Re-read the first five lines.*
   What kind of scene do these lines describe?
2. *Read again the next four lines.*
   Who is the visitor the writer most wants?
3. *Read the second verse.*
   What is the poet offering to the robin?
4. *Read verse three.*
   What does this verse tell you about the robin?
5. *Look right through the poem quickly.* Pick out the number of times the word *come* is used.
   Read these lines.
   What do they tell you about the writer's feelings about the robin?

* * * * *

The Robin in Superstition and Legend

Superstitions

In some parts of Britain people believe that if a robin comes into your house or pecks against a closed window, this means that there will be a death in the family. But in other parts they believe the opposite. There they believe that a robin in the house or at the window means that there will be a new baby soon.

In all parts of the country people have long believed that it is very unlucky to kill a robin. If you catch a robin and put him in a cage, that will bring disaster on you. William Blake, the poet, tells us this:

> A Robin Redbreast in a cage
> Puts all Heaven in a rage.

Another way to risk bad luck is to harm a robin's nest or

take its eggs. Here are two old country rhymes which warn against doing these things:

> The robin and the wren
> Are God Almighty's cock and hen.
> Him that harries their nest,
> Never shall his soul have rest.

> The robin and the redbreast,
> The robin and the wren,
> If ye take out o' their nest,
> Ye'll never thrive again.

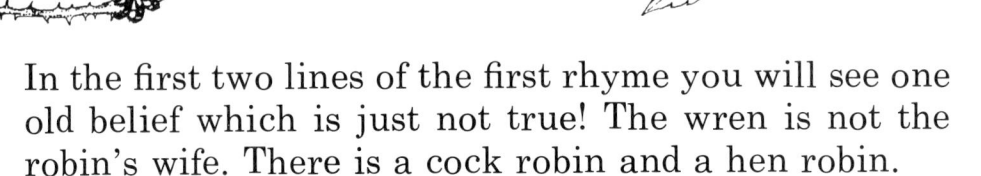

In the first two lines of the first rhyme you will see one old belief which is just not true! The wren is not the robin's wife. There is a cock robin and a hen robin.

One other superstition was that you had to feed the robin in bad weather if you wanted to have good luck. You had to do so even if you had to risk him coming into your house to eat!

Some experts think that the reason for all of these superstitions can be traced to another old belief. This belief was that when a robin came across a dead body he set to work and tried to cover it up with leaves and bits of moss. These experts also think that this belief is where the story of "Babes in the Wood" comes from.

Legends

In pagan times the robin was a sacred bird. It was the bird of Thor, the Viking god of thunder. If any mortal dared harm the robin, Thor would take dreadful revenge on that person.

In some parts of England there is a legend that tells of the robin's pity for mankind. The legend says that the robin was full of pity for those souls condemned to live forever in Hell. Every day the robin took a drop of water in its beak and flew down to try to put out the great fires of Hell. It flew so near to the flames that its breast feathers were scorched. Because it was so hot down there, the robin still feels cold in winter. That is why he shelters inside buildings if he can.

Another legend says that the wren stole fire from Hell and gave it to mankind. When the wren reached earth with its precious cargo the little bird was on fire. The brave robin burnt its breast putting out the flames.

A well-known Welsh legend is that the robin tried to pull the thorns out of the crown on Christ's head when he was on the Cross. His feathers were stained by the blood of Christ.

Questions

Main ideas (See pages 58 to 60.)

1. *Read the superstitions over again and then finish off these two sentences.*
   (a) It is unlucky to . . . .
   (b) It is lucky to . . . .
2. *Read the legends and finish off this sentence.*
   Never harm a robin or . . . .
3. Why does the robin have a red breast?
   Read the legends to find the answers.

Finding proof

> The North wind doth blow
> And we shall have snow.
> What will the robin do then poor thing?
> He'll sit in a barn
> to keep himself warm,
> And hide his head under his wing, poor thing.

This is a well-known nursery rhyme about the robin. One of the legends tells why the robin does this. Which legend? What reason does the legend give?

Little Robin Roughneck

1. That pretty, little robin redbreast, that cheery, cheeky, bobbing, wee chappie is just a feathered THUG! That's the truth! Never mind all the fancy stories! Forget about the bright-eyed little bobber who is everybody's friend. In reality it is one of the tetchiest, most bad-tempered, most selfish creatures in the whole animal kingdom.

2. We may imagine that the poor robin's sad little song is a comfort to us in the dead of winter. It reminds us that spring will come again. But that is not at all what it really means. In reality it is a blunt and belligerent warning. It says to all other birds, "This is my territory. Keep out! That means you!" Its home patch means more to the robin than anything else. Its song is a clear NO ENTRY sign, as clear as the Berlin Wall.

3. Woe betide the bird that hops over the boundary. The robin puffs itself up to its full height of 13 cm and pushes out its chest like some red badge of courage. Trespassers should pay attention to this red flag of danger. If this display does not frighten off the invader, then all-out war comes next. The

robin will fight to the death. In fact the robin has been known to fight furiously with its own reflection.

4. But if this is the truth, how did this pugnacious little bird ever become part of our Christmas? Surely Christmas is about peace and goodwill? The GPO is to blame! During Queen Victoria's reign it became the fashion to send Christmas cards. These cards were delivered by "robins". These "robins" were postmen. They got their name from the bright red uniforms they wore at that time.

5. So there!

Questions

Understanding the passage

1. What is the robin's true character?
2. Why does it sing?
3. What does the robin use its breast for?
4. What is the connection between the robin and Christmas?

Alphabetical order, context clues, dictionary

Here is a list of the meanings of some of the words in the passage. The paragraph number is given to help you. *Find the word which you think matches the meaning. When you have done that, put your words into the correct alphabetical order and then use your dictionary to check your words.*

(a) fact, truth   (1)
(b) gets angry very easily   (1)
(c) ready to wage war, warlike   (2)
(d) amount of land he owns   (2)
(e) people who go on to other people's property without permission   (3)
(f) picture seen in a mirror   (3)
(g) always ready to fight, warlike   (4)

17 Main Ideas

In Book 1, Inspector I. N. Quire, gave you these rules:

1. Look at all of the ideas in the passage.
2. Decide which idea includes the others.
3. The idea which says what the whole passage is about, is the main idea.

These rules do not change, but, like the cases the Inspector works on, the examples are different and some are more difficult.

Examples

1. Here is a short passage. Once again we sent it to the Inspector to ask for his expert opinion. We asked for the main idea and for him to say why. He sent it back with the main idea underlined and his reason for choosing it.

Toss a coin in the air and it will fall back down. Fire up a rocket on November 5th and down it comes again. Miss the peg with your coat, and it will fall until the floor stops it. <u>The force of gravity pulls everything down to earth.</u>

Reason
That is the main idea because it says what the important point in the passage is. The other sentences are only examples of what gravity does. The main idea includes all of the other ones. It says what the whole paragraph is about.

2. We also sent this passage to our Inspector. He underlined the main idea again and said why.

<u>The Inspector examined the picture carefully.</u> It showed a tall, well-built man in an old jacket. The

man had dark hair and his face showed the signs of many a battle. He had a broken nose, scars above both eyes and on one cheek.

Reason
That is the main idea because it says what the passage is all about. The other sentences give details of what the Inspector saw in the picture.

Exercises

1. *Here is a short passage. Below it are some possible main ideas. Pick out the one which you think really is the main idea. Say why you think so.*

The frogs were singing in their deep-throated way. The young otters were sliding down the bank into the river. The goose was watching over them like a life-guard. Even the snakes were contented as they lay asleep in the heat of the sun. It was a wonderful June day. The kind of day when it's good to be alive.

(a) Lots of animals were swimming.
(b) Frogs were singing.
(c) It was a beautiful day.
(d) It was such a fine day that all the animals were joyful.
(e) The animals were all happy.

2. Here is another passage. Pick out the main idea and say why you chose it.

The house stood all on its own and there was no sign of life. It was a fearful place. The windows had broken shutters over them. The door stood slightly ajar. It was a creepy, almost ghostly place in the moonlight. As the wind blew, the shutters creaked and clattered. The door squealed open a bit further and revealed nothing but more darkness inside.

3. Once again read this passage, pick out the main idea and say why you chose it.

As the daylight returned they saw that the house was really just a deserted, half-ruined shepherd's cottage. Imagination can play funny tricks, especially in the dark. It can change a perfectly ordinary, old house into a home for ghosts. It can make ordinary things seem strange and alarming. After all, the wind does make open shutters and doors move. Hinges which have not seen oil for a long time do creak and squeak and squeal.

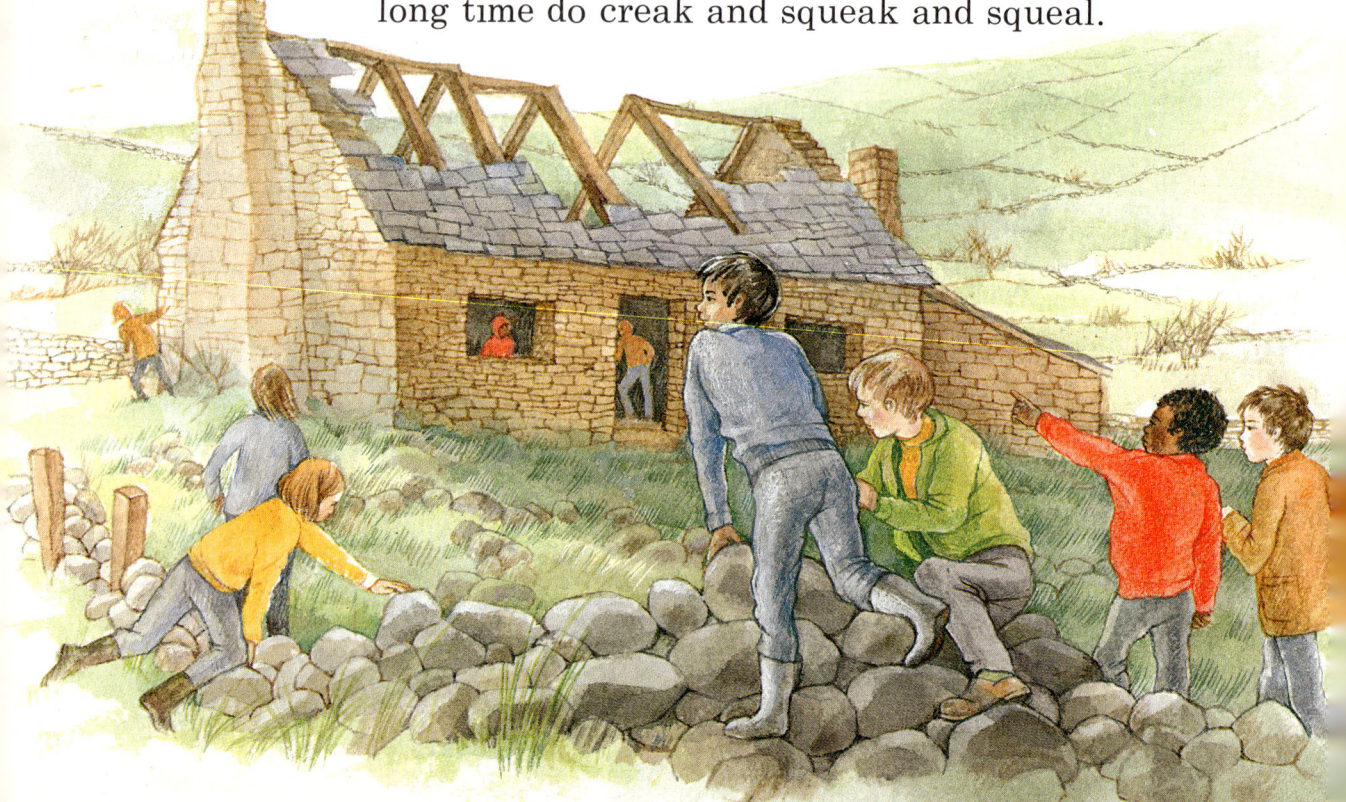

18 Christmas Customs

1. Let's start with Christmas Day itself. No one is sure exactly when Christ was born. At one time Christmas was held in January or in March. December 25th was a special day before Christian times. The Romans held feasts and gave presents to one another on that day. Later still the Normans came to Britain. They brought with them a very wild custom of a special day called "The Feast of Fools". On that day, December 25th, masters became servants and servants became masters. Boys were made Lords for one day. Things got so wild that in 1555 a law was passed to ban this custom. Some of the customs still go on to-day. On the Feast of Fools actors performed wild plays. Nowadays we have pantomimes at Christmas. In the pantomimes the hero is played by a girl, the nasty woman is played by a man and there is often a funny horse with men inside it. The actors used to do all these things on the Feast of Fools. After the Feast of Fools was banned, Christmas Day began to be held on December 25th in its place.

2. What about Boxing Day? Boxing Day is the day after Christmas Day. It got its name from a custom of not quite so long ago. Tradesmen used to bring round boxes to collect tips from rich people. They also hoped that they would get a drink of punch at the houses. Boxing Day is also Saint Stephen's Day. That was the day when King Wenceslas looked out in the carol. Saint Stephen was a disciple of Jesus. He was stoned to death on that day long ago because he was a Christian.

3. Christmas crackers began in 1860. A sweet maker called Tom Smith started wrapping sweets in fancy paper. Then he began to put jokes and charms in them. Later still he put a banger in to make them crack when they were pulled. At first crackers were called "bangs of expectation".

Questions

Context clues

Here is a list of other Christmas customs. Can you work out what each one is? *Match each one with one of the drawings.* There are six drawings.

1. At one time these were dances performed holding hands.
2. These came from the religion of the Vikings. For good luck save a bit of this year's one to kindle next year's.
3. A boar's head used to be in the centre of the table. Four hundred years ago this bird was brought from America. It is now the main part of the Christmas feast.
4. In Britain long ago the Druids thought that it should be cut with a golden knife. If it was hung above the door it would stop storms from harming the house. We still hang it above doors. A boy has the right to kiss any girl who stands under it. For luck the girl should pick one of the berries and throw it over her shoulder.

5. He comes from the days of the plays performed on the Feast of Fools. Saint Nicolas Day is really on 6th December. Saint Nicolas lived about the year 400. He was supposed to have brought three boys back to life. He became the children's saint. In Holland children get presents on 6th December.

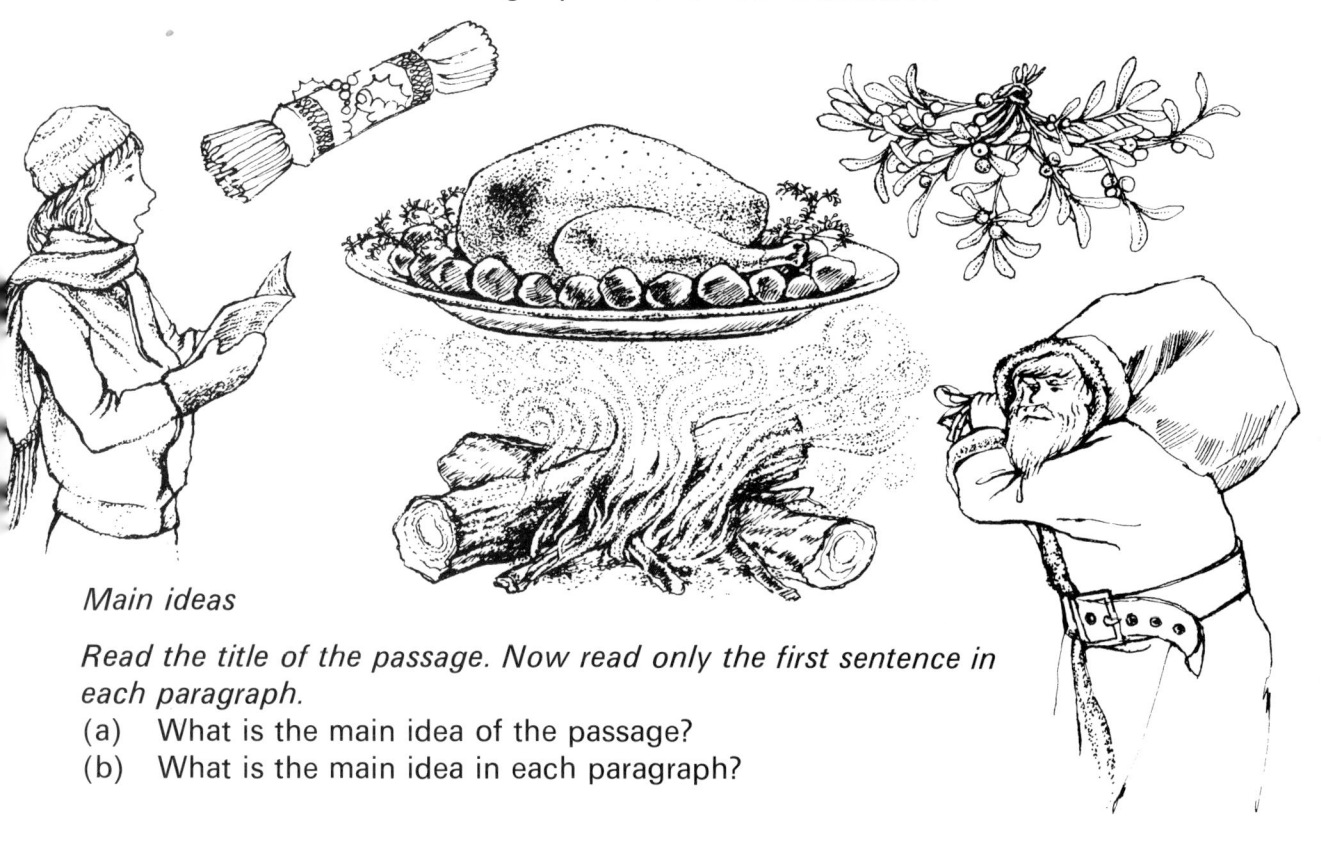

Main ideas

Read the title of the passage. Now read only the first sentence in each paragraph.
(a) What is the main idea of the passage?
(b) What is the main idea in each paragraph?

Details (See pages 67 to 69.)

1. *Read the first two paragraphs.* Which of these sentences are *true*? Which are *false*? Why?
   (a) The Romans held Christmas in February.
   (b) For the Romans December 25th was a feast day when they exchanged gifts.
   (c) December 25th was a feast day for the Normans.
   (d) "The Feast of Fools" was a day when things were done the wrong way round.
   (e) In 1555 a law was passed to ban Christmas Day.
   (f) Christmas pantomimes still contain things which began in "The Feast of Fools".
   (g) Christmas Day is held on December 25th because that was the day when Christ was born.

2. *Read the third paragraph.* Which of these sentences are *true*? Why?
   (a) Boxing Day is the day after the Feast of Stephen.
   (b) Boxing Day gets its name from the boxes men carried for tips on that day.
   (c) King Wenceslas saw St Stephen being stoned to death.
   (d) St Stephen was killed for his beliefs.

Sequence

1. *Read the last paragraph. Put these sentences in the same order as the things which happened in the paragraph.*
   1. Bangers were put inside the wrapping paper.
   2. A maker of sweets wrapped some of his products in paper.
   3. The first real crackers had an odd name.
   4. Little objects and jokes were wrapped inside crackers.

2. Here is a recipe for a hot drink.
   Work out the recipe so that you will be able to make it.

   Chocolate Mint Sizzler

   Look at the recipe.
   1. Put a mugful of milk into a pan.
   2. Heat the milk carefully and mix in a dessert spoon of drinking chocolate.
   3. Add a chocolate peppermint cream.
      Stir the mixture until the sweet melts.

   Now look at the pictures. Put them in the right order.

   (a)   (b)   (c)

19 The Story Of Skiing

1. Skiing can be great fun. Thousands of people now enjoy the sport of skiing. When the snow falls and hills are steep enough, out come the skis. Some people prefer cross-country skiing. Most people like skiing downhill and that is called alpine skiing.

2. Skiing began hundreds of years ago. In Norway and Sweden skis were used for cross-country travel in winter. Some stories of this way of travel are as old as 2000 years. In 1765 a book on how to ski well was printed in Norway. The book was for soldiers in Norway who had to move around in the winter snow in their country.

3. Modern ski sport began in Norway. In 1850 in Norway a man called Norheim invented skis which are like the ones we still use. He also tried out different ways of binding boots to these skis. That was a very important change. Unless the boot and the ski are held tightly together modern skiing is impossible. Good bindings give better control of the skis. With his new skis and bindings he showed new ways of turning and jumping on skis. Ski clubs were formed all over Norway. Competitions were held for jumping, cross country and slalom. Modern skiing had begun as a sport.

4. In Europe and North America there are many mountains and people there wanted to try skiing. In the high Alps in Austria more changes happened. In 1896 Mathias Zdarsky, an Austrian, wrote a new book on skiing. He had invented shorter skis and even better ways of binding boot and ski together.

5.   His bindings were stronger because they were metal ones. The better bindings made control easier still. Turning the skis was easier too.

5.   From the early 1900s skiing became a popular holiday sport in the winter. Ski resorts grew up in Norway and in Austria, France, Switzerland and Italy. The design of skis was improved even more. In the 1930s Rudolph Lettner, another Austrian, invented steel edges for skis. These edges helped the skier to get a better grip when he was turning.

6.   Even more changes have taken place in the last twenty years. Skis are now made from strong plastics instead of wood. Bindings are even stronger and safer. Modern bindings are of the "step-in" sort. With these bindings there are no problems of bending and fastening. The skier just steps in and pushes his heel down. The bindings then clamp the boots tightly in the skis.

7.   Most people ski for the fun of it. Only a few experts take part in races. Most enjoy alpine skiing—skiing down mountain slopes. A lot of people do still prefer cross-country skiing.

Questions

Understanding the passage

1. Pick out the dates mentioned in the passage. What happened on these dates?
2. Look at each date. Why was it important?
3. What are the two most popular kinds of skiing? What is the difference between them?
4. What other kind of skiing competition is mentioned?

20 Details

Inspector I. N. Quire will tell you that details matter a lot in his detective work. It is not enough for him to know that he is looking for a man. He needs details. He needs to know about age, size, hair colour, what the face is like, clothes and so on. In reading we also need details. If we have a main idea, we need details to support it. For example, if the main idea is that a house looked creepy, we need to know what made it look creepy.

Examples

1. A policeman told the Inspector that he had seen a man in the street who was behaving strangely. (Main idea)

    "How?" asked the Inspector. "Was he standing on his head and singing the National Anthem backwards?"

    "No," said the policeman. "He walked past the jewellers six times. Each time he looked at some rings in the window, then he peered into the shop. Next he looked up and down the street and then walked away. He was also carrying a bag which looked heavy."

    "Right. Now I see what you mean," replied the Inspector.

    "But it's no use just giving me an idea like that. I need to know the details."

2. Sometimes the Inspector gets information the other way round. That is, he gets the details and has to work out the main idea for himself.
   Here are some details he was given about a case:
   (a) No windows were broken and the door had not been forced.
   (b) The burglar alarm had its wires cut outside the building.
   (c) The telephone cable had been cut outside the building.
   (d) There were no strange finger prints.
   (e) Nobody heard anything unusual.
   (f) Only the most valuable things had been taken.
   Inspector I. N. Quire had this to say:
   "All of these details point to one main idea. The main idea is that the crime was done by expert, professional thieves."

Exercises

1. *Here is a main idea.*
   Belle Starr was the leader of a gang of bandits.
   Pick out which of these details support that main idea.
   (a) Myra Belle Shirley was born in 1848 into a respectable family.
   (b) At eighteen she ran away from home to work in the saloons in Dallas, Texas.
   (c) She fell into bad company.
   (d) She married Tim Starr, a horse thief.
   (e) Belle was the leader of the gang and planned their raids.
   (f) Stories say that she led the gang on their raids.
   (g) In the stories, she rode her black mare, Venus, and wore velvet riding clothes and a long feather in her hat.

2. *Here is a main idea.*
   Colt's revolver made great changes in the Wild West.
   Now read this passage and pick out the details which support that main idea.

Samuel Colt's new gun did not fire only one shot at a time. Instead it had a cylinder which moved round each time a shot was fired. That was why the gun was called a revolver. In the West it was said that any man who had one was equal to any other man in a fight. Size and strength did not count for so much in these fights. The Colt six-shooter made all men equal in the Wild West.

3. *Here is a picture.* The title (or main idea) of the picture is: "A peaceful scene in the country."
   Look at the picture and pick out the details which support that main idea.

Inspector I. N. Quire's Rules for Details

1. Details are important. A main idea without details might not mean very much.
2. Sometimes just the details can give you the main idea.
3. Be careful to check which of the details do support the main idea. Some may not.

21 Athletes On Skis

1. The really expert skiers are the ones you see on television in the Olympic Games or the World Cup races or jumps. They take part in different kinds of racing and jumping events. These men and women have to be superb skiers and they must be very brave indeed. There are races for men and for women. But women do not take part in ski jumping contests.

2. There are different kinds of races. Perhaps the most thrilling to watch is the downhill race. Downhill skiers race down narrow and steep slopes to see who can get from top to bottom in the shortest time. They travel at terrific speeds of more than 120 kph. The courses twist sharply and have bumps where the racers take off through the air. Usually only fractions of a second separate the skiers. To win they must take daring risks and ski flat out all the time.

3. Slalom and giant slalom races need great skill. In these races the skiers have to weave their way round and between poles. They must go as fast as they can and still take the right course. Going the wrong way disqualifies a skier. Slalom races are on short courses with the poles placed close together. For giant slalom races the course is longer and the poles are further apart. The very best skiers usually choose to race either in downhill or in slalom. Not many are equally good at both slalom and downhill.

4. Then there is ski jumping. It is perhaps the most thrilling of all. The skier takes off down a specially built, steep runway. At the end he shoots off into the air, flies through space and lands on the hillside below. The winner is the skier who can fly the furthest and makes the most perfect flight and landing. Ski jumpers usually do not take part in downhill or slalom races. Racers do not usually take part in jumping.

5. There are also cross-country skiing races. They are not as thrilling or as spectacular as downhill slalom and jumping. But cross-country skiing is very tiring and does need skill too. In the Olympic Games there is a special sort of cross country race called the biathlon. The skiers travel across country and each one carries a rifle. At set places they have to get out of their skis and shoot at targets. The winner is the one who goes fastest and makes a very good score at shooting.

6. Although only a few skiers take part in these events, thousands of other people can enjoy skiing for fun. Skiing also helps to bring pleasure to thousands during the long, cold days of winter. These days there are many ski resorts in many countries. In Britain there are some ski resorts in the north of Scotland.

Questions

Finding proof

Here are some sentences. *Read each one and decide whether it is* true *or* false. *If you think it is* false, *say why.*
1. Men and women take part in all kinds of racing and jumping events.
2. Women have downhill races.
3. Downhill racers ski fast down a straight course.
4. Slalom racers have to be very skilful.
5. Giant slalom racers are always the best downhill racers too.
6. To win at ski jumping a skier has to jump further and be more graceful than the other skiers.
7. Cross country skiing is less dangerous than downhill and slalom skiing.
8. You do not have to be an expert to enjoy skiing.

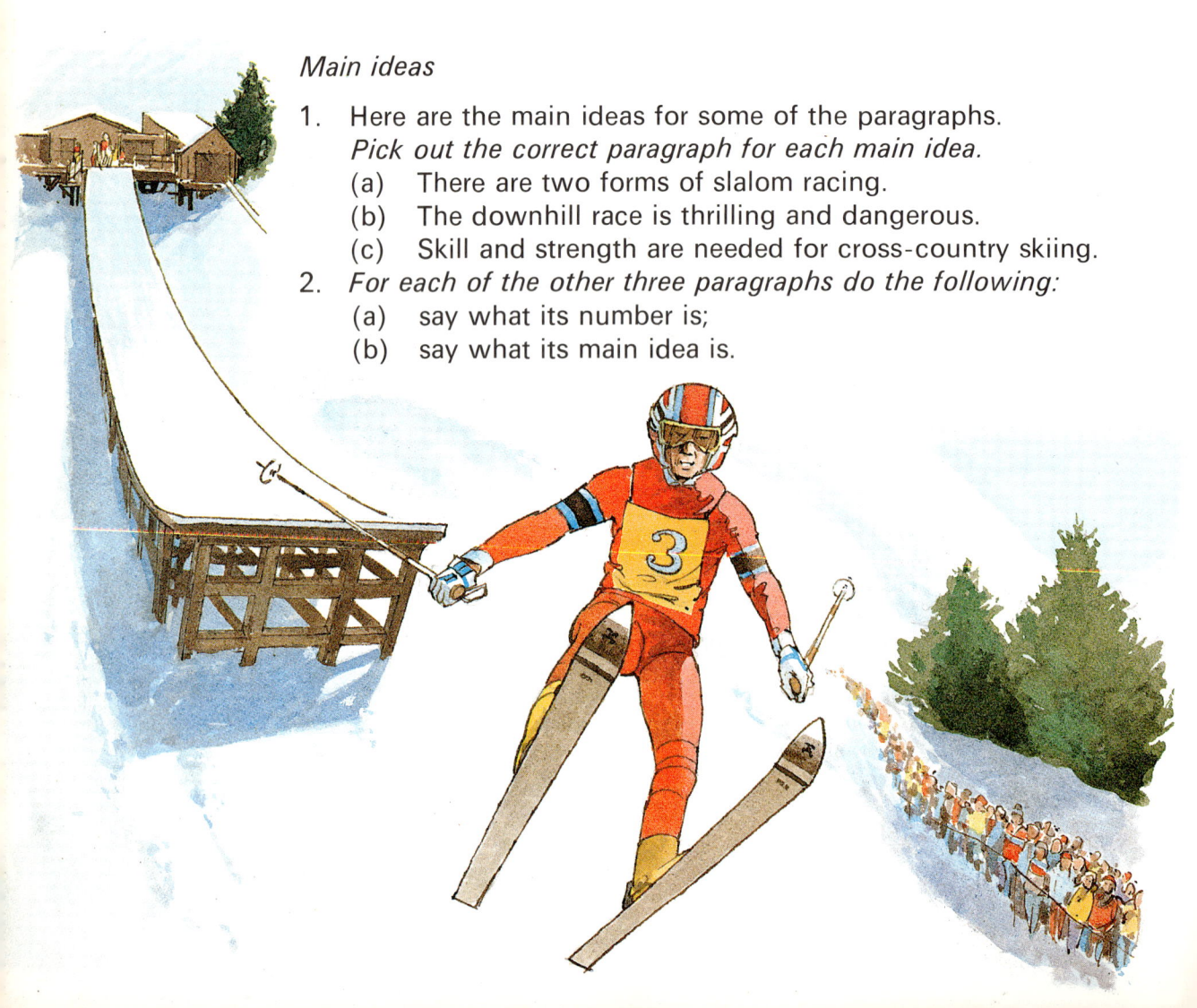

Main ideas

1. Here are the main ideas for some of the paragraphs.
   Pick out the correct paragraph for each main idea.
   (a) There are two forms of slalom racing.
   (b) The downhill race is thrilling and dangerous.
   (c) Skill and strength are needed for cross-country skiing.
2. *For each of the other three paragraphs do the following:*
   (a) say what its number is;
   (b) say what its main idea is.